Holiday cookies

and other festive treats

Linda Collister

with photography by William Reavell

Holiday cookies
and other festive treats

RYLAND
PETERS
& SMALL

LONDON NEW YORK

Senior Designer Toni Kay
Editor Céline Hughes
Production Gemma John
Art Director Leslie Harrington
Publishing Director
Alison Starling

Food Stylist Rachel Miles
Prop Stylist Liz Belton
Indexer Hilary Bird

First published in the US in 2008
by Ryland Peters & Small, Inc.
20–21 Jockey's Fields
London WC1R 4BW
www.rylandpeters.com

10 9 8 7 6 5 4 3 2 1

Library of Congress Cataloging-in-
Publication Data

Collister, Linda.
 Holiday cookies and other festive
treats / Linda Collister with photography
by William Reavell.
   p. cm.
 Includes index.
 ISBN 978-1-84597-702-3
 1. Cookies. 2. Holiday cookery. I. Title.
 TX772.C387 2008
 641.5'68--dc22

2008016964

Author's acknowledgments
I would like to thank the following for their
help: Barbara Levy, Céline Hughes, William
Reavell, Toni Kay, Liz Belton, Rachel Miles,
and Stevie and Dan Hertz.

Notes
• All spoon measurements are
level, unless otherwise specified.
• All eggs are medium, unless otherwise
specified. It is generally recommended that
free-range eggs be used. Uncooked or partially
cooked eggs should not be served to the very
young, the very old, those with compromised
immune systems, or to pregnant women.
• Ovens should be preheated to the specified
temperature. Recipes in this book were tested
using a regular oven. If using a convection
oven, follow the manufacturer's instructions
for adjusting temperatures.
• To sterilize preserving jars, wash them in hot,
soapy water and rinse in boiling water. Place
in a large pan, then cover with hot water.
With the lid on, bring the water to a boil and
continue boiling for 15 minutes. Turn off the
heat, then leave the jars in the hot water
until just before they are to be filled. Sterilize
the lids for 5 minutes. Jars should be filled
and sealed while they are still hot.

Contents

Introduction

In our house, you *smell* Christmas first: the warm, spicy sweetness of festive baking, the fresh green-ness of newly cut pine. And the celebrations begin as we prepare to make edible gifts and treats. Many families develop their own traditions and make the same favorites every year. But ours is a family of different residences, nationalities, backgrounds, and interests, so each year we try something new.

The easiest recipes in this book—the decorated cookies—are also the most impressive. These are based on the crisp, gently spiced, and fragrant cookies popular in Advent markets across northern Europe for many centuries. Supermarkets and kitchen stores sell the tools you'll need, and these make great stocking stuffers. You can buy fancy cutters in seasonal shapes, writing icing pens, edible decorations, ribbons, and threads for hanging. Children love to be involved, so wrap them in aprons and get them into the kitchen. If you don't want to put the finished cookies on the tree itself (they're miniature works of art after all!), you can hang them elsewhere: from ropes of tinsel, stripped twigs, thin copper pipes, or wooden rods. Another easy project, suitable for children, is the Truffles (page 68): they are not too rich and are good gifts for teachers.

The more sophisticated cookies—the German Lebkuchen (page 19), French Chocolate Fingers (page 31), Dutch Vanilla Butter Cookies (page 23)—also make good presents. Pack them into pretty boxes or tins (my children cover old coffee tins in gift wrap) or wrap them in cellophane and lots of colored ribbon. Label them with storage instructions, a list of ingredients in case of allergies, and the "eat-by" date (the recipes will give you all the information you need).

With a bit of advance planning, you can get ahead with festive meals. I make a big batch of Cranberry and Basil Relish (page 87) to go with our Thanksgiving turkey and keep a jar for Christmas, when we have another turkey with all the traditional and well-loved trimmings. Like the Ginger Fruit Relish (page 88), it is also good for livening up the leftovers, the cold meats, ham, and cheese served in our house from Boxing Day until New Year or until the turkey is no more.

On Christmas day itself I serve a selection of savory nibbles to soak up the pre-lunch Champagne. These can be made ahead, frozen, then warmed before serving—try the Chile Cheese Gougères (page 76) or some rich and crumbly Cheese Palmiers (page 75). Any leftovers are good served with soup. The Grissini (page 80) are bread sticks served with dips or wrapped in prosciutto. The easiest possible recipes are also the most irresistible—Spicy Nuts and Marinated Olives (both page 83).

It's fun when friends and family drop by unexpectedly to deliver cards and presents, but I've often been caught on the hop. So I've learned to prepare and hide a stash of homemade cakes that double as dessert. I now appreciate why my grandmother, born into a big family in the nineteenth century, said she could face the festivities as long as she had a ham, a matured cheese, and a large fruitcake in the larder. Brownies (pages 44–47) are always a winner and can be transformed into an easy dessert if served warm with ice cream and a drizzle of melted chocolate. A cut-and-come-again cake such as the Lemon Pecan (page 56) or the quick and simple Chocolate Brandy (page 52) will be popular with everyone. But for sheer versatility muffins (pages 60–65) are wonderful—for breakfasts and brunches, mid-afternoon snacks, and midnight feasts—and they can be made in advance and kept in the freezer. Meanwhile, for an indulgent New Year's Day breakfast, try some little Brioches (page 59).

Start baking and bring the fun and fragrance of Christmas into your house!

Holiday
cookies

GOOD TO EAT AND FUN TO DECORATE, THEN HANG FROM
FINE RED OR SILVER RIBBONS. TRY DECORATING WITH
GLACÉ ICING MADE FROM SIFTED CONFECTIONERS' SUGAR
MIXED WITH A LITTLE HONEY INSTEAD OF WATER.

Iced honey and cinnamon cookies

2½ cups all-purpose flour

2 teaspoons ground cinnamon

1 teaspoon apple pie spice

1½ sticks unsalted butter, chilled and diced

6 tablespoons honey

To decorate

royal or glacé icing, or writing icing pens, silver balls, thin ribbon (see Suppliers, page 94)

shaped cookie cutters

2 baking sheets, lightly greased

MAKES ABOUT 24, DEPENDING ON SIZE OF CUTTERS

Put the flour, cinnamon, and apple pie spice into the bowl of a food processor. Pulse a couple of times just to mix. Add the diced butter and pulse until the mixture looks like fine crumbs. Add the honey and process until the mixture comes together to make a soft dough.

Remove the dough from the bowl, shape into a ball, and wrap in plastic wrap. Chill until firm, about 30 minutes. The dough can be kept in the fridge, tightly wrapped, for up to 5 days.

Remove the dough from the fridge, unwrap, and roll out on a lightly floured work surface until about ¼ inch thick. Dip the cookie cutters in flour and cut out shapes from the dough. Gather up the trimmings and re-roll, then cut more shapes. Arrange the shapes slightly apart on the prepared baking sheets. If using as decorations, use a skewer or toothpick to make a small hole at the top of each shape large enough to thread a ribbon through. Chill for 10–15 minutes until firm.

Preheat the oven to 350°F.

Bake in the preheated oven for 10–12 minutes until just firm. Let cool for 3 minutes on the baking sheets, then transfer to a wire rack until completely cold. Decorate with royal icing (page 15) or glacé icing (page 16), or use a writing icing pen. Add silver balls while the icing is wet, but wait until the icing is thoroughly dry before threading with ribbon. Store the cookies in an airtight container and eat within 5 days.

LIGHTLY GOLDEN AND WELL SPICED, THESE ARE RICHER THAN THE USUAL GINGERBREAD MEN, BUT FOR A DEEPER COLOR REPLACE THE SOFT LIGHT BROWN SUGAR WITH DARK BROWN. DECORATE TO YOUR HEART'S DESIRE.

Gingerbread shapes

2½ cups all-purpose flour
1 teaspoon baking soda
1 tablespoon ground ginger
1 teaspoon ground cinnamon
1½ sticks unsalted butter
1 cup firmly packed light brown sugar
¼ cup light molasses

To decorate
royal or glacé icing, or writing icing pens, ribbons, edible silver balls (see Suppliers, page 94)

shaped cookie cutters

several baking sheets, lined with baking parchment

MAKES ABOUT 18 MEDIUM OR 12 LARGE

Sift the flour, baking soda, ginger, and cinnamon into a bowl.

Put the butter, sugar, and molasses into a pan large enough to hold all the ingredients. Set over low heat to melt very gently. Remove the pan from the heat and add all the sieved ingredients. Mix thoroughly with a wooden spoon to make a firm dough. Leave until cool enough to handle. Turn out onto a work surface and knead gently to make a neat ball, then wrap in plastic wrap and chill until firm, about 20 minutes.

Preheat the oven to 350°F.

Remove the dough from the fridge, unwrap, and roll out on a lightly floured work surface until ¼ inch thick. Dip the cookie cutters in flour and cut out shapes. Gather up the trimmings and re-roll, then cut out more shapes. Arrange slightly apart on the prepared sheets. Bake in the oven for 8–10 minutes until lightly browned. If using as decorations, use a skewer or toothpick to make a small hole at the top of each shape large enough to thread a ribbon through. Let cool completely, then decorate with royal icing (see below) or glacé icing (page 16), or use a writing icing pen. Add silver balls while the icing is wet, but wait until the icing is thoroughly dry before threading with ribbon. Store the shapes in an airtight container and eat within 1 week.

Royal icing—This icing will harden as it dries. It can be colored with a few drops of icing food coloring and is easily piped using a parchment paper piping bag fitted with a fine tip or simply with the tip of the bag snipped off. Sift 1½ cups confectioners' sugar into a bowl and stir in an egg white to make an icing that is stiff but can be piped or spread. Spoon into the piping bag and snip off the point when ready to decorate.

THESE WELL-FLAVORED COOKIES ARE SIMPLE TO MAKE AND ARE IDEAL DECORATIONS. PICK YOUR FAVORITE COOKIE CUTTERS, THEN ONCE THEY ARE BAKED, HAVE FUN ICING AND FINISHING.

Iced star cookies

1¼ sticks unsalted butter, at room temperature

½ cup sugar

finely grated zest and freshly squeezed juice of 1 unwaxed lemon

⅓ cup cream cheese

2¼ cups all-purpose flour

a good pinch of salt

1 teaspoon apple pie spice

To decorate

royal or glacé icing, or writing icing pens, edible silver balls, ribbons (see Suppliers, page 94)

a star-shaped cookie cutter

2 baking sheets

MAKES ABOUT 24 4-INCH STARS

Beat the butter with the sugar and lemon zest using a wooden spoon or electric mixer. Beat in 2 teaspoons of the lemon juice and all the cream cheese. Sift in the flour, salt, and apple pie spice and work in. When thoroughly combined, remove the dough from the bowl, shape into a ball, and wrap in plastic wrap. Chill until firm, 30 minutes. The dough can be kept in the fridge, tightly wrapped, for up to 1 week.

Preheat the oven to 350°F.

Remove the dough from the fridge, unwrap and roll out on a lightly floured work surface until ¼ inch thick. Dip the cookie cutter in flour and cut out shapes. Gather up the trimmings and re-roll, then cut out more shapes. Arrange slightly apart on the baking sheets. If using as decorations, use a skewer or toothpick to make a small hole at the top of each shape large enough to thread a ribbon through. Bake for 12–15 minutes until just turning golden brown at the edges. Remove from the oven, let cool for 3 minutes, then transfer to a wire rack until completely cold. Decorate with royal icing (page 15) or glacé icing (see below), or use a writing icing pen. When firm, thread with ribbons. Store in an airtight container and eat within 5 days.

Glacé icing—Made with confectioners' sugar and water, plus a little coloring if you like. It will dry firm but not as hard as royal icing. Sift ¼ cup confectioners' sugar into a bowl. Stir in water or lemon juice, a teaspoon at a time, to make a thick icing that can be piped. To be able to spread the icing, add a little more water to make a consistency that runs slowly off the back of the wooden spoon when it is held up.

IN GERMANY, IT WOULDN'T BE CHRISTMAS WITHOUT LEBKUCHEN. FOLLOWING A TRADITION THAT DATES BACK TO THE MEDIAEVAL MONASTERIES, THEY ARE MADE FROM HONEY AND SEVEN SPICES TO REPRESENT THE SEVEN DAYS OF GOD'S CREATION. THIS IS MY FAVORITE VERSION, BASED ON MERINGUE AND NUTS AND WITH JUST SIX SPICES—CRISP AND LIGHT BUT DENSELY FLAVORED.

Lebkuchen

¼ **cup almonds (not blanched)**

1 oz bittersweet chocolate, coarsely chopped

2 tablespoons mixed candied peel, very finely chopped

½ **teaspoon ground cinnamon**

½ **teaspoon ground ginger**

¼ **teaspoon freshly grated nutmeg**

¼ **teaspoon ground black pepper**

¼ **teaspoon ground cloves**

¼ **teaspoon ground allspice**

2 extra-large egg whites

1 cup confectioners' sugar, sifted

To decorate

7 oz good bittersweet chocolate, chopped

2 baking sheets, lined with baking parchment

MAKES 16

Preheat the oven to 300°F.

Put the almonds and chopped chocolate into the bowl of a food processor and process until the mixture looks like fine crumbs. Mix with the finely chopped peel and all the spices.

Put the egg whites into a spotlessly clean, grease-free bowl and, using an electric whisk or mixer, whisk until stiff peaks form. Gradually whisk in the confectioners' sugar, then whisk for another minute to make a very stiff, glossy meringue. Sprinkle the spice mixture over the top and gently fold in with a large metal spoon.

Take tablespoons of the mixture and drop them on the prepared baking sheets, spacing them well apart to allow for spreading. Using a round-bladed knife, spread out each mound to a disk about 3 inches across. Bake in the preheated oven for 15–20 minutes, until pale gold and firm.

Remove the baking sheets from the oven, set on a wire rack, and let cool completely. When cold, peel the lebkuchen off the baking parchment.

To decorate, melt the chocolate in a heatproof bowl set over a pan of steaming but not boiling water. Do not let the base of the bowl touch the water. Stir gently until melted, then remove from the heat. Spread some melted chocolate over one side of each lebkuchen with a palette knife, then let set on a sheet of baking parchment.

Store in an airtight container and eat within 4 days.

TRADITIONALLY MADE FOR THE CHRISTMAS HOLIDAYS, THESE DARK SPICY COOKIES CAN BE LEFT PLAIN OR DECORATED WITH WHITE ICING—YOU CAN USE READY-MADE ICING WRITING PENS FOR THIS.

Swedish pepper cookies

1½ cups all-purpose flour

½ teaspoon baking soda

1 teaspoon ground cinnamon

1 teaspoon ground ginger

½ teaspoon ground black pepper

freshly grated zest of
1 unwaxed orange

¾ cup sugar

1 stick unsalted butter,
chilled and diced

1 egg, lightly beaten

1 tablespoon molasses

a star-shaped cookie cutter

several baking sheets, greased

MAKES ABOUT 15

Put all the ingredients in a food processor and blend until the mixture forms a soft dough.

When thoroughly combined, remove the dough from the processor, shape into a ball, and wrap in plastic wrap. Chill until firm, about 1 hour.

Remove the dough from the fridge, unwrap, and roll out on a lightly floured work surface until about ¼ inch thick. Dip the cookie cutter in flour and cut out shapes. Gather up the trimmings and re-roll, then cut out more shapes. Arrange the cookies slightly apart on the prepared baking sheets and chill for 10 minutes.

Preheat the oven to 325°F.

Bake in the preheated oven for 10–12 minutes until dark golden brown and firm.

Let cool for 5 minutes, then transfer to a wire rack until completely cold. Store in an airtight container and eat within 1 week or freeze for up to 1 month.

THESE ARE RICHER THAN SHORTBREAD YET EASY TO MAKE (THERE'S NO ROLLING AND CUTTING) AND FLAVORED WITH VANILLA BEAN SEEDS. IF YOU PREFER YOU CAN USE A TEASPOON OF REALLY GOOD PURE VANILLA EXTRACT. THE DOUGH CAN BE STORED IN AN AIRTIGHT CONTAINER IN THE FRIDGE FOR UP TO 5 DAYS BEFORE BAKING.

Dutch vanilla butter cookies

2 sticks unsalted butter, at room temperature

⅞ cup sugar

1 vanilla bean, about 3 inches

1 extra-large egg

1¼ cups all-purpose flour

½ teaspoon baking powder

a good pinch of salt

demerara or raw cane sugar, to decorate

1–2 baking sheets

MAKES ABOUT 24

Preheat the oven to 350°F.

Put the butter and sugar into the bowl of a food processor. Split the vanilla bean lengthwise, scrape out the tiny black seeds with the tip of a knife, and add them to the bowl. Beat until light and creamy. Beat in the egg, beating until very light and fluffy.

Sift the flour, baking powder, and salt into the bowl and mix in using the lowest possible speed.

Flour your hands, then take a walnut-size piece of dough and roll it into a ball. Set on a baking sheet. Repeat with the rest of the dough, arranging the cookies well apart to allow for spreading. Lightly sprinkle the tops with sugar—there's no need to flatten the cookies—then bake in the preheated oven for 15–18 minutes until lightly golden and slightly darker around the edges.

Let the cookies cool on the baking sheets for 2 minutes, then transfer to a wire rack until completely cold. Store in an airtight container and eat within 5 days or freeze for up to 1 month.

THIS RECIPE WAS VERY POPULAR WHEN I WAS SMALL AND
PEANUT BUTTER WAS CONSIDERED RATHER EXOTIC —MY
FATHER BROUGHT OUR FIRST JAR HOME AS A TREAT FROM
A TRIP TO CHICAGO—BUT I'VE ADDED THE CHUNKS OF
BITTERSWEET CHOCOLATE AS I LIKE THE CONTRAST TO
THE SALTY SWEETNESS OF THE COOKIE MIX. LOOK FOR ALL-
NATURAL PEANUT BUTTER WITHOUT ADDED SUGAR OR FAT.

Peanut butter choc chunkies

1¼ cups all-natural chunky
peanut butter

1 cup firmly packed light
brown sugar

½ teaspoon pure vanilla extract

1 extra-large egg, beaten

⅓ cup all-purpose flour

3½ oz bittersweet chocolate,
coarsely chopped

*2 baking sheets, lined with
baking parchment*

MAKES 24

Preheat the oven to 350°F.

Put the peanut butter, sugar, vanilla extract, and egg into a mixing
bowl and mix thoroughly with a wooden spoon. Work in the
flour and the chocolate, then use your hands to bring the dough
together—it will be a bit crumbly.

Take a tablespoon of dough and roll it into a ball. Set on a prepared
baking sheet. Repeat with the rest of the dough, arranging the
chunkies well apart to allow for spreading, then slightly flatten with
the back of a fork. Bake in the preheated oven for 12–15 minutes
until just firm and golden and slightly colored around the edges.

Remove the baking sheets from the oven and set on a wire rack to
cool completely. Lift the cooled chunkies off the baking sheets and
store in an airtight container. Best eaten within 1 week.

POSSIBLY THE WORLD'S RICHEST CHOCOLATE
COOKIE, MADE WITH AN AWFUL LOT OF GOOD
CHOCOLATE (BOTH MELTED AND IN CHUNKS MIXED
IN WITH WALNUTS), PLUS JUST A LITTLE FLOUR,
THEN DECORATED WITH MORE CHOCOLATE.

Triple chocolate cookies

10½ oz bittersweet chocolate,
coarsely chopped

½ stick unsalted butter,
at room temperature

2 extra-large eggs,
at room temperature

⅔ cup sugar

½ teaspoon pure vanilla extract

3 tablespoons all-purpose flour

¼ teaspoon baking powder

1 cup walnut pieces

To decorate

2 oz bittersweet chocolate,
coarsely chopped

*2 baking sheets, lined with
baking parchment*

MAKES 24

Preheat the oven to 350°F.

Put 7 oz of the chopped bittersweet chocolate in a heatproof bowl set over a pan of steaming but not boiling water. Do not let the base of the bowl touch the water. Stir gently until melted, then remove from the heat. Gently stir in the butter.

Put the eggs, sugar, and vanilla extract into the bowl of an electric mixer and whisk until very thick and mousselike and the whisk leaves a ribbonlike trail when lifted—this will take 3–4 minutes.

Sift the flour and baking powder into the bowl and gently fold in with a large metal spoon. Add the melted chocolate mixture and fold in. When almost combined add the remaining 3½ oz chopped bittersweet chocolate and the walnut pieces and mix in.

Take tablespoons of the mixture and drop them on the prepared baking sheets, spacing them well apart to allow for spreading. Bake in the preheated oven for 10 minutes until barely set.

Remove from the oven and set the baking sheets on a wire rack until the cookies have cooled completely.

To decorate, melt the chocolate in a heatproof bowl set over a pan of steaming water (as above). Dip a fork or teaspoon into the chocolate and drizzle over the cookies. Leave to set, then store in an airtight container and eat within 1 week.

THESE SWEET, ALMOND-RICH COOKIES ARE LIKE SOFT,
CHEWY AMARETTI. SERVE WITH COFFEE AT THE END OF
A SPECIAL MEAL; A BOX OF THEM MAKES A LOVELY GIFT.

Sardinian almond cookies

1 lb almond paste
1 cup slivered almonds
2 egg whites
a scant ½ cup confectioners' sugar

2 baking sheets, lined with baking parchment

MAKES 30

Preheat the oven to 300°F.

Break up the almond paste and put in a food processor. Process briefly until the paste is finely chopped. Add ⅔ cup of the almonds, the egg whites and sugar and process until the mixture forms a thick, smooth paste.

Take tablespoons of the mixture and drop them on the prepared baking sheets, spacing them well apart to allow for spreading. Scatter the remaining almonds over the top. Bake in the preheated oven for about 25 minutes until light golden brown.

Remove from the oven and let cool completely on the baking sheets. Store in an airtight container and eat within 1 week. These cookies don't freeze very well.

Variation—Replace the almonds (in the mixture and for sprinkling) with pine nuts.

HERE ARE SOME ELEGANT PIPED CHOCOLATE COOKIES,
FINISHED WITH BITTERSWEET CHOCOLATE, THAT REALLY
DO MELT IN THE MOUTH. PIPING BAGS AND TIPS ARE
AVAILABLE FROM KITCHEN STORES AND THE BAKEWARE
DEPARTMENTS OF LARGE STORES, AS WELL AS ONLINE
(SEE SUPPLIERS, PAGE 94), AND CAN BE USED TO PIPE
MERINGUES, WHIPPED CREAM, AND COOKIES.

French chocolate fingers

1½ sticks unsalted butter,
at room temperature

¼ cup sugar

½ teaspoon pure vanilla extract

¼ cup unsweetened cocoa powder

1¼ cups all-purpose flour

½ teaspoon baking powder

To decorate

3 oz bittersweet or white
chocolate, coarsely chopped

a piping bag, fitted with a fluted tip

*2 baking sheets, lined with
baking parchment*

MAKES ABOUT 30

Preheat the oven to 350°F.

Put the butter, sugar, and vanilla extract into a bowl and beat with
a wooden spoon or electric mixer until light and fluffy. Sift in the
cocoa, flour, and baking powder and fold in until thoroughly combined.

Spoon the mixture into the piping bag. Pipe the mixture onto the
prepared baking sheets in fingers about 3½ inches long, spacing them
well apart to allow for spreading. Bake in the preheated oven for
about 15 minutes or until slightly colored around the edges.

Remove from the oven and let cool completely on the baking sheets—
the cookies are quite fragile.

To decorate, melt the chocolate in a heatproof bowl set over a pan of
steaming but not boiling water. Do not let the base of the bowl touch
the water. Dip a fork or teaspoon into the chocolate and drizzle over
the cold cookies. Let set, then store in an airtight container and eat
within 5 days.

VERY GLAMOROUS INDEED—THESE ULTRA CRISP SNAPS ARE
LOVELY WITH COFFEE, ICE CREAM, OR SORBET. BUT THE BEST
WAY TO SERVE THEM IS TO DIP THE ENDS IN CHOCOLATE THEN
FILL THEM WITH WHIPPED, BRANDY-LACED CREAM.

Lacy brandy snaps

6 tablespoons unsalted butter

⅓ cup plus 1 tablespoon sugar

3 tablespoons light corn syrup
or light molasses

scant ⅔ cup all-purpose flour

1 teaspoon ground ginger

2 teaspoons brandy

*several baking sheets, lined with
baking parchment*

*several wooden or stainless steel
spoons with thick handles*

MAKES 20

Preheat the oven to 350°F.

Put the butter, sugar, and corn syrup in a small pan and set over gentle heat.
Stir with a wooden spoon until melted and smooth. Remove the pan from
the heat. Mix the flour with the ginger and stir into the melted mixture
along with the brandy to make a smooth and thick batter.

Take tablespoons of the mixture and drop onto the prepared baking sheets,
spacing the snaps about 4 inches apart to allow for spreading (there is no
need to spread out the mixture). Do not put more than 5 snaps on each
sheet. Bake 1 sheet at a time in the preheated oven until bubbly and golden
brown, 7–10 minutes.

Remove the sheet from the oven and let cool for exactly 1 minute, then
quickly lift each snap off the sheet with a palette knife or spatula and gently
roll around thick wooden or stainless steel spoon handles (I use a ladle) to
make a hollow roll. The roll will firm up rapidly as it cools so you need to
work quickly while it is warm and pliable. If the mixture has set before it
can be shaped, return the sheet to the oven for 1 minute until pliable again.

Leave the rolls to cool on the spoon handles until they are firm enough
to hold their shape, then gently slide off, set on a wire rack, and let cool
completely. While the first batch is cooling, bake the second and so on.
Store in an airtight container and eat within 1 week.

Brandy snap baskets—Drape the warm snaps over small oranges to form cup
shapes. Leave until set and firm, then lift off and turn the right way up.
Fill, just before serving, with ice cream.

THIS RECIPE FOR SNOWY-WHITE, RICH ALMOND COOKIES
COMES FROM A CZECH FRIEND, BUT I'VE EATEN POLISH,
GERMAN, AND DUTCH VERSIONS, AND MY MOTHER-IN-LAW
MAKES SOMETHING SIMILAR DURING HANNUKAH.

Czech almond crescents

1 cup blanched almonds

½ cup confectioners' sugar, plus extra to dust

1 stick unsalted butter, chilled and diced

2–3 drops pure almond extract

¼ cup all-purpose flour

2 baking sheets, well greased

MAKES 24

Put the almonds and sugar in a food processor and blend until the mixture becomes a fine, sandy powder. Add the butter, almond extract, and flour and process until the mixture forms a ball of smooth dough.

Carefully remove the dough from the machine, wrap in plastic wrap, and chill for about 20 minutes or until firm. The dough can be kept in the fridge, tightly wrapped, for 24 hours.

When ready to cook, preheat the oven to 325°F.

Remove the dough from the fridge, unwrap, and pull off a rounded teaspoon of the dough. Roll it with your hands to make a sausage shape about 3 inches long. Curve the dough into a crescent and set on a prepared baking sheet. Repeat with the rest of the dough, arranging the crescents well apart on the sheets. Bake in the preheated oven for 15–18 minutes until the edges are barely colored.

Let cool on the baking sheets for 2 minutes, then carefully transfer to a wire rack to cool completely. Just before serving, dust with plenty of confectioners' sugar. Store in an airtight container and eat within 1 week. These cookies are fragile and, while they can be frozen, they tend to break easily.

Variation—Melt 2 oz good-quality bittersweet chocolate and dip one end of each cooled crescent into the chocolate. Leave to set on baking parchment. Sprinkle the plain end with confectioners' sugar before serving.

SABLÉS ARE TO THE FRENCH WHAT SHORTBREAD IS TO SCOTS—MADE FROM THE BEST BUTTER WITH A LIGHT HAND, AND JUST AS WELL LOVED. THESE ARE STUDDED WITH PISTACHIOS ALTHOUGH YOU COULD ALSO USE FINELY CHOPPED, LIGHTLY TOASTED PECANS OR ALMONDS, AND CUT INTO SIMPLE DISKS OR FANCY SHAPES AS YOU LIKE.

Pistachio sablés

1 stick unsalted butter, at room temperature

½ teaspoon pure vanilla extract

½ cup plus 1 tablespoon confectioners' sugar, sifted

1 extra-large egg yolk

1¼ cups all-purpose flour

a good pinch of baking powder

a good pinch of salt

¼ cup shelled pistachios, finely chopped

demerara or raw cane sugar, to sprinkle

shaped cookie cutters

2 baking sheets, lined with baking parchment

MAKES ABOUT 24

Beat together the butter, vanilla extract, and confectioners' sugar with an electric mixer (starting on low speed) or a wooden spoon. When the mixture is very light and fluffy, beat in the egg yolk.

Sift the flour, baking powder, and salt into the bowl and work in with a wooden spoon. When almost combined, add the nuts and work in well.

Remove the dough from the bowl, shape into a ball, and wrap in plastic wrap. Chill until firm, about 15 minutes. The dough can be kept in the fridge, tightly wrapped, for up to 3 days.

When ready to cook, preheat the oven to 325°F.

Remove the dough from the fridge, unwrap, and roll out on a lightly floured work surface until about ¼ inch thick. Dip the cookie cutters in flour and cut out shapes. Gather up the trimmings and re-roll, then cut out more shapes. Arrange slightly apart on the prepared baking sheets and sprinkle with a little demerara or raw cane sugar. Bake in the preheated oven for 17–20 minutes until barely colored and lightly golden around the edges.

Remove the baking sheets from the oven and set on a wire rack. Let cool for 5 minutes until firm enough to transfer to a cooling rack. Store in an airtight container and eat within 1 week or freeze for up to 1 month.

EXCELLENT FOR DUNKING IN COFFEE OR A GLASS OF VIN
SANTO, THESE CRISP, NUTTY BISCOTTI ARE GIVEN A FESTIVE
TWIST WITH SWEETENED DRIED CRANBERRIES.

Almond biscotti

1 stick unsalted butter,
at room temperature

⅔ cup sugar

1 teaspoon pure vanilla extract

2 extra-large eggs, at room
temperature, beaten

2 cups all-purpose flour

a good pinch of salt

½ teaspoon baking powder

1 cup sweetened dried
cranberries

1 cup blanched almonds,
roughly chopped

*2 baking sheets, lined with
baking parchment*

MAKES 24

Preheat the oven to 350°F.

Beat together the butter, sugar, and vanilla extract with an electric mixer
or wooden spoon, until light and fluffy. Gradually beat in the eggs.

Sift the flour, salt, and baking powder into the bowl and work in with a
wooden spoon. When almost combined, add the cranberries and almonds
and mix thoroughly to make a soft dough.

Turn out the dough onto a floured work surface and divide into 2 equal
portions. Using well floured hands, lift a portion of dough onto each
prepared baking sheet and shape into a brick 10 x 3½ inches. Bake in
the preheated oven for about 25 minutes until golden and just firm.

Remove the baking sheets from the oven, set on a wire rack, and let cool
for 10 minutes. Using a serrated bread knife, slice the logs (still on the
sheets) on the diagonal about ⅓ inch thick. Put, cut-side down, on the
sheets and return to the oven. Bake for 10 minutes until starting to color.

Remove the baking sheets from the oven, put on a wire rack, and let cool
completely. Store in an airtight container and eat within 3 weeks.

CRISP, CRUNCHY CHOCOLATE COOKIES STUDDED WITH
CHUNKS OF BITTERSWEET CHOCOLATE AND PECANS—
LOVELY WITH ICE CREAM AS WELL AS HOT DRINKS.

Chocolate chip biscotti

3 extra-large eggs,
at room temperature

1¼ cups firmly packed light
brown sugar

finely grated zest of
1 unwaxed orange

1 stick unsalted butter, melted

2⅓ cups all-purpose flour

1 tablespoon baking powder

generous ¼ cup unsweetened
cocoa powder

1 cup pecan pieces

3½ oz bittersweet chocolate,
coarsely chopped

*2 baking sheets, lined with
baking parchment*

MAKES ABOUT 36

Preheat the oven to 350°F.

Put the eggs, sugar, and orange zest in the bowl of an electric mixer and whisk until very frothy. Whisk in the melted butter.

Sift the flour, baking powder, and cocoa into the bowl and mix with a wooden spoon. Work in the pecans and chopped chocolate.

When thoroughly combined, turn out the dough onto a floured work surface and divide into 2 equal portions. Using well floured hands, lift a portion of dough onto each prepared sheet and shape into a brick 12 x 3 inches—they will spread in the oven. Bake in the preheated oven for 25–30 minutes until just firm when pressed.

Remove the baking sheets from the oven (you can turn off the oven) and let cool completely.

When ready to continue, reheat the oven to 350°F. Using a serrated bread knife, slice the logs (still on the sheets) on the diagonal about ⅓ inch thick. Put, cut-side down, on the sheets and return to the oven. Bake for 10 minutes until crisp and dry.

Remove the baking sheets from the oven, put on a wire rack, and let cool completely. Store in an airtight container and eat within 3 weeks.

Brownies, bars, and cakes

THERE ARE NO NUTS BUT PLENTY OF CHOCOLATE IN THESE MOIST, RICH BROWNIES. FOR THE MOST INTENSE FLAVOR, USE TOP-QUALITY WHITE AND BITTERSWEET CHOCOLATE.

Triple chocolate brownies

7 oz bittersweet chocolate,
coarsely chopped

7 tablespoons unsalted butter,
at room temperature, cubed

1 cup plus 2 tablespoons sugar

½ teaspoon pure vanilla extract

4 extra-large eggs,
at room temperature

½ cup all-purpose flour

⅔ cup unsweetened cocoa
powder

3½ oz white chocolate,
coarsely chopped

a 10 x 8-inch baking pan, greased and baselined with parchment paper

MAKES 24

Preheat the oven to 350°F.

Melt the chocolate in a heatproof bowl set over a pan of steaming but not boiling water. Do not let the base of the bowl touch the water. Stir occasionally until melted, then remove the bowl from the heat and let cool until needed.

Beat the butter, sugar, and vanilla extract with an electric mixer or wooden spoon until light and fluffy, then gradually beat in the eggs, beating well after each addition.

Stir in the melted chocolate, then sift the flour and cocoa into the bowl and mix in.

Transfer the mixture to the prepared pan and spread evenly. Scatter the chopped white chocolate over the top, then bake in the preheated oven for 20 minutes, or until a toothpick or skewer inserted halfway between the sides and the center comes out slightly moist but not sticky with uncooked batter.

Remove the pan from the oven and set on a wire cooling rack. Let cool completely, then cut into 24 pieces. Store in an airtight container and eat within 4 days.

I'M OFTEN ASKED FOR A BROWNIE RECIPE WITHOUT FLOUR, AND THIS ONE IS QUITE WONDERFUL. IT IS INCREDIBLY RICH AND STICKY, AND IS BEST SERVED WITH A SCOOP OF ICE CREAM. AS WITH A LOT OF CHOCOLATE CAKES, IT IS AT ITS BEST MADE A DAY IN ADVANCE.

Flourless sticky brownies

10½ oz good bittersweet chocolate, coarsely chopped

2 sticks unsalted butter, diced

3 extra-large eggs, at room temperature

1½ cups firmly packed soft light brown sugar

½ cup ground almonds

1 teaspoon baking powder

1 cup walnut pieces

a 10 x 8-inch baking pan, greased and baselined with parchment paper

MAKES 24

Preheat the oven to 350°F.

Melt the chocolate and butter in a heatproof bowl set over a pan of steaming but not boiling water. Do not let the base of the bowl touch the water. Stir frequently until melted, then remove the bowl from the heat and let cool until needed.

Put the eggs and sugar into the bowl of an electric mixer and whisk until very pale, thick, and mousselike, about 3 minutes.

Using a large metal spoon, fold in the melted chocolate mixture. Combine the ground almonds with the baking powder and mix in, followed by the walnuts.

Transfer the mixture to the prepared pan and spread evenly. Bake in the preheated oven for about 40 minutes until just firm to touch and a toothpick or skewer inserted about halfway between the sides and the center comes out clean.

Remove the pan from the oven and set on a wire rack. Let cool completely, then cut into 24 pieces, or if possible, wrap the entire brownie in foil or waxed paper and leave for a day before cutting. Store in an airtight container and eat within 5 days.

IF YOU WANT ALL THE FRAGRANCES AND FLAVORS OF
A CHRISTMAS CAKE BUT DON'T WANT THE WORK, THIS
MELT-AND-MIX CAKE IS A GREAT ALTERNATIVE. IT'S GOT
DRIED FRUIT, SPICES, AND ALCOHOL BUT IS LOW IN FAT,
MADE WITHOUT EGGS, AND CAN BE SERVED WITH JUST
A DUSTING OF CONFECTIONERS' SUGAR.

Cider fruit squares

½ stick unsalted butter

1 cup firmly packed light
brown sugar

⅔ cup raisins

⅔ cup golden raisins

⅓ cup roughly chopped
dried apricots

¾ cup apple cider

1 teaspoon apple pie spice

1 teaspoon ground ginger

1⅔ cups fine wholewheat flour,
sifted to remove bran

2 teaspoons baking powder

a good pinch of salt

confectioners' sugar, to dust

*a 10 x 8-inch baking pan, greased
and baselined with parchment paper*

MAKES 24

In a saucepan large enough to hold all the ingredients, put the
butter, sugar, raisins, chopped apricots, cider, apple pie spice,
ground ginger, and ¾ cup water. Bring to a boil, stirring frequently,
then reduce the heat and simmer gently for 2 minutes.

Remove the pan from the heat and let cool. Meanwhile, preheat the
oven to 350°F.

Sift the flour, baking powder, and salt into the pan, adding any fine
pieces of bran left in the sieve. Mix with a wooden spoon until
thoroughly combined.

Pour the mixture into the prepared pan and spread evenly. Bake in
the preheated oven for about 25 minutes until a good golden brown
and firm to the touch.

Remove from the oven and set on a wire rack to cool completely.
The cake tastes best if covered tightly and left overnight before
cutting. Cut into 24 squares and dust with confectioners' sugar.
Store in an airtight container and eat within 1 week.

LEMON SQUARES AND BARS ARE EVER-POPULAR AND A
STAPLE OF MANY A BAKE SALE AND COFFEE MORNING.
BUT FOR CHRISTMAS I LIKE TO MAKE THIS RICHER FRENCH
VERSION, USING THICK CREAM RATHER THAN FLOUR IN
THE FILLING—AND IT'S JUST AS EASY TO MAKE.

Lemon squares

For the base
1¼ cups all-purpose flour
¼ cup confectioners' sugar
finely grated zest of
½ unwaxed lemon
1 stick unsalted butter,
chilled and diced

For the topping
3 extra-large eggs,
at room temperature
1½ cups confectioners' sugar,
sifted, plus extra to dust
finely grated zest of
2 unwaxed lemons
freshly squeezed juice
of 4 lemons
½ cup heavy cream

an 8-inch square baking pan,
lined with aluminum foil

MAKES 12

Preheat the oven to 350°F.

To make the base, put the flour, confectioners' sugar, and lemon zest into the bowl of a food processor and process for a few seconds until combined. Add the butter and process to make fine crumbs.

Tip into the prepared baking pan and press onto the base with your fingers to make an even layer. Bake in the preheated oven for about 25 minutes until firm and pale golden. Remove from the oven and let cool while you make the topping.

To make the topping, crack the eggs into a bowl and beat with a small whisk until broken up. Add the sugar and whisk until thoroughly combined. Add the lemon zest and juice and mix thoroughly, then work in the cream.

Return the pan to the oven and slightly pull out the shelf just enough so you can pour the filling into the pan. Gently push the shelf back into place, then close the door and reduce the temperature to 325°F. Bake for about 25 minutes until just firm.

Put the pan on a wire cooling rack and let cool completely, then cover lightly and chill overnight. Use the foil to lift the whole square out of the pan, then cut into 12 pieces. Dust with confectioners' sugar and serve. Store in an airtight container in the fridge and eat within 3 days.

A RICH CHOCOLATE TREAT TO SERVE IN THIN SLICES WITH COFFEE OR WHIPPED CREAM FOR DESSERT. THERE'S NO BAKING INVOLVED AS IT'S MADE FROM MELTING VERY GOOD BITTER CHOCOLATE WITH BUTTER, THEN MIXING WITH WHISKED EGGS AND SUGAR AND FLAVORING WITH BRANDY (OR WALNUT LIQUEUR IF YOU CAN FIND IT), TOASTED WALNUTS, AND THE BEST DRIED CRANBERRIES YOU CAN FIND.

Chocolate brandy cake

9 oz bittersweet chocolate, coarsely chopped

2 sticks unsalted butter, diced

9 oz graham crackers

2 extra-large eggs, at room temperature

¼ cup sugar

1⅔ cups walnut halves, lightly toasted

¾ cup sweetened dried cranberries

¼ cup brandy or walnut liqueur

unsweetened cocoa powder, to dust

a 9-inch springform pan, lined with plastic wrap

MAKES 16 SLICES

Melt the chocolate and butter in a heatproof bowl set over a pan of steaming but not boiling water. Do not let the base of the bowl touch the water. Stir frequently until melted, then remove the bowl from the heat and let cool until needed. Coarsely crush the graham crackers with a rolling pin or in a food processor.

Using an electric or rotary whisk, beat the eggs with the sugar until very thick and mousselike and the whisk leaves a ribbonlike trail when lifted out of the bowl. Whisk in the melted chocolate mixture.

Coarsely chop two-thirds of the walnuts and carefully fold in with the cranberries, brandy, and the crushed crackers.

Spoon into the prepared pan and spread evenly. Decorate with the rest of the walnut halves. Cover the top of the pan with plastic wrap and chill for at least 4 hours or overnight.

When ready to serve, unclip the pan and remove the plastic wrap. Dust with cocoa and serve cut into thin slices. Store in an airtight container in the fridge for up to 1 week.

THE SWEDISH FESTIVAL OF ST LUCIA ON DECEMBER 13TH HAS A COMPLEX HISTORY. OVER TIME IT HAS ABSORBED A PAGAN WINTER SOLSTICE FESTIVAL, THE FEAST OF ST. NICHOLAS, AND A MODERN FESTIVAL OF LIGHT. THIS GOLDEN CAKE, MADE FOR THE FESTIVAL, USES SAFFRON FOR THE FLAVOR AND THE SYMBOLISM OF THE COLOR. SERVE WITH WHIPPED CREAM AND RED FRUIT CONSERVE (PAGE 92).

Swedish saffron cake

½ cup milk
2 sticks slightly salted butter
1 teaspoon saffron threads
2 extra-large eggs,
at room temperature
1 cup sugar
1⅔ cups all-purpose flour
2 teaspoons baking powder
confectioners' sugar, to dust

a 9-inch springform pan, greased, baselined with parchment paper, and sprinkled with dried bread crumbs or ground almonds

MAKES ONE MEDIUM CAKE

Heat the milk with the butter until melted and steaming hot but not boiling. Remove the pan from the heat and sprinkle in the saffron. Cover the pan and let infuse for 1 hour.

When ready, preheat the oven to 350°F.

Put the eggs into the bowl of an electric mixer and whisk until just frothy. Whisk in the sugar and continue whisking until very thick and mousselike and the whisk leaves a ribbonlike trail when lifted out of the bowl.

Gently fold in the just-warm saffron mixture. Sift the flour and baking powder into the bowl and fold in gently with a large metal spoon—the mixture will look hopeless at first but it will combine after a minute.

Pour into the prepared pan and bake in the preheated oven for 35–40 minutes until the cake is a good golden brown, slightly shrunk from the sides of the pan, and firm to touch.

Put on a wire rack and unclip the pan. Let cool completely, then serve dusted with confectioners' sugar. Store in an airtight container and eat within 4 days. Not suitable for freezing.

THIS FESTIVE CAKE, BASED ON A FRENCH QUATRE-QUARTS OR POUND CAKE, IS A RICH LEMON CAKE STUDDED WITH PECANS AND DRIED CRANBERRIES. FOR A SPECIAL TOUCH, DECORATE WITH FRESH CRANBERRIES DIPPED IN BEATEN EGG WHITE, ROLLED IN SUGAR, AND LEFT TO DRY FOR 24 HOURS ON BAKING PARCHMENT.

Lemon pecan cake

2 cups pecan halves

1½ cups sweetened dried cranberries

1½ cups all-purpose flour

2 sticks unsalted butter, at room temperature

1 cup sugar

finely grated zest and juice of 1 unwaxed lemon

4 extra-large eggs, at room temperature, separated

a good pinch of salt

1 teaspoon baking powder

confectioners' sugar, to dust

frosted cranberries (optional), see introduction above

ribbon, to decorate

a 9-inch springform pan, greased and lined with parchment paper

MAKES ONE MEDIUM CAKE

Preheat the oven to 300°F.

Put the pecans and cranberries in a bowl with a couple of tablespoons of the flour and toss well to break up any clumps of fruit. Set aside until needed.

Beat the butter until very soft and creamy using an electric mixer or wooden spoon. Add the sugar and lemon zest and beat well until fluffy. Beat in the egg yolks, one at a time, then beat in the lemon juice.

Sift the remaining flour, the salt, and baking powder into the bowl and gently fold in using a large metal spoon. Add the pecan-cranberry mixture and fold in.

Whisk the egg whites in a spotless, greasefree bowl until stiff peaks form, then fold into the cake mixture in 3 batches.

Spoon into the prepared pan and spread evenly. Bake in the preheated oven for about 1¼ hours or until lightly golden and a toothpick inserted into the center of the cake comes out clean (if there is damp batter on the toothpick return the cake to the oven and bake for about 5 minutes longer and test again). Set the pan on a wire rack and let cool completely. Remove the cake from the pan and discard the parchment paper. Wrap in fresh paper and store in an airtight container for at least 24 hours before cutting. Serve dusted with confectioners' sugar (you can use a stencil in the shape of a star or tree) and tied with a ribbon. Decorate with frosted cranberries if desired (see introduction above). Eat within 2 weeks or freeze for up to 1 month.

IF YOU WANT WARM BRIOCHES ON THE TABLE FOR BREAKFAST, YOU CAN MAKE AND SHAPE THE DOUGH THE NIGHT BEFORE, READY FOR BAKING IN THE MORNING. NORMALLY THE DOUGH GETS THREE RISINGS BUT MY SON CAME UP WITH THIS SIMPLER AND MUCH QUICKER VARIATION.

Chocolate brioches

4 cups all-purpose flour

¼ oz active dry yeast

1 teaspoon salt

1½ sticks unsalted butter, diced

¼ cup sugar

3 extra-large eggs, at room temperature

⅔ cup milk, lukewarm

3½ oz bittersweet chocolate, coarsely chopped

beaten egg, to glaze

a 12-cup muffin pan, silicone or well-greased nonstick metal

MAKES 12

Put the flour, yeast, and salt in the bowl of a large electric mixer and mix by hand. Add the butter and rub into the flour with your fingertips until the mixture looks like fine crumbs. Mix in the sugar. Beat the eggs with the milk until thoroughly combined, then add to the flour mixture. Using the dough hook attachment of the mixer, mix the ingredients on low speed until you get a heavy, sticky dough. Scrape down the sides, then knead the dough in the machine on low speed for 5 minutes until glossy, very smooth and soft. If you don't have a food mixer, mix the ingredients as above, then knead the dough by hand. Cover and let rise at normal room temperature (not too warm) until doubled in size, 1½–2 hours.

Turn out the risen dough onto a lightly floured work surface. Punch down, then work in the chopped chocolate, kneading gently for about 1 minute. Divide the dough into 12 equal portions. Pinch off a marble-size ball from each portion and roll into a smooth, neat ball. Shape the rest of the portion into a neat ball and drop into the muffin pan. Flour your index finger and push into the center of the dough in the pan, then place the smaller ball over this hole. Repeat with the remaining portions of dough. Slip the pan into a large plastic bag, slightly inflate, then let rise until doubled in size, about 1 hour in a warm kitchen or overnight in the fridge.

When ready to continue, preheat the oven to 400°F.

Uncover the brioches and lightly brush with beaten egg to glaze. Bake in the preheated oven for 18–20 minutes until firm and a good golden color. Let cool for a minute for the crust to firm up, then carefully turn out onto a wire rack. Eat warm or let cool completely, then store in an airtight container and eat within 24 hours or freeze for up to 1 month.

NOT AS SWEET AS SOME MUFFINS, THESE ARE GOOD
FOR BRUNCH AND BREAKFAST ALONG WITH SOME
GOOD COFFEE DURING THE HOLIDAYS WHEN THE
HOUSE IS FULL OF PEOPLE.

Christmas mini-muffins

1¼ cups all-purpose flour

1 teaspoon baking powder

a pinch of salt

¼ cup sugar

finely grated zest of
½ unwaxed orange

½ cup pecan pieces, coarsely
chopped, plus 2 tablespoons,
to decorate

1½ tablespoons raisins

½ cup fresh or frozen
cranberries (no need to thaw)

1 extra-large egg, beaten

½ stick unsalted butter, melted

½ cup milk

confectioners' sugar, to dust

*mini-muffin pans lined with foil
mini-muffin cases, or use double
cases set on a baking sheet*

MAKES 30

Preheat the oven to 350°F.

Sift the flour, baking powder, and salt into a mixing bowl.
Stir in the sugar, orange zest, chopped pecans, and raisins.

Put the cranberries into the bowl of a food processor and chop
roughly. Stir into the flour mixture.

Combine the beaten egg with the melted butter and milk and
stir into the flour mixture with a wooden spoon.

Spoon the mixture into the foil cases using 2 teaspoons, then
decorate with the extra pecans. Bake in the preheated oven
for 12–15 minutes until barely golden and firm to the touch.

Turn out onto a wire rack. Serve warm, dusted with
confectioners' sugar. When cold, store in an airtight container
and eat within 2 days.

FOR PARTIES, BRUNCHES, AND OFFICE TREATS, SMALL, ONE-BITE MUFFINS ARE ALWAYS POPULAR AND EASILY TRANSPORTED. THESE CAN BE LEFT PLAIN, DUSTED WITH CONFECTIONERS' SUGAR OR DECORATED WITH EXTRA NUTS OR CHOCOLATE CHIPS. USE CONTRASTING CHOCOLATE CHIPS FOR THE BEST EFFECT.

Chocolate mini-muffins

½ stick unsalted butter, at room temperature

¼ cup sugar

1 extra-large egg, beaten

½ cup sour cream

⅓ cup white, bittersweet, or milk chocolate chips, plus extra to decorate

⅞ cup all-purpose flour

¼ cup unsweetened cocoa powder

½ teaspoon baking powder

½ teaspoon baking soda

a pinch of salt

confectioners' sugar, to dust

mini-muffin pans lined with foil mini-muffin cases, or use double cases set on a baking sheet

MAKES ABOUT 30

Preheat the oven to 350°F.

Put the butter and sugar in a mixing bowl and beat with a wooden spoon until fluffy. Beat in the egg until thoroughly combined. Finally, beat in the sour cream followed by the chocolate chips.

Sift the flour, cocoa, baking powder, baking soda, and salt into the bowl and combine without overmixing.

Spoon the mixture into the foil cases using 2 teaspoons, then decorate with a few extra chocolate chips. Bake in the preheated oven for 12–15 minutes until firm to the touch.

Let cool on a wire rack and serve dusted with confectioners' sugar. Store in an airtight container and eat within 2 days.

SPICY, STICKY AND UTTERLY IRRESISTIBLE. ALWAYS
POPULAR WITH CHILDREN, YOU CAN GET THEM TO
DECORATE THE MUFFINS WITH WRITING ICING PENS
AND GIVE THEM AS GIFTS TO THEIR FRIENDS.

Gingerbread mini–muffins

7 tablespoons unsalted butter

2 tablespoons molasses

2 tablespoons honey

⅔ cup firmly packed dark brown sugar

½ cup milk

1¼ cups all-purpose flour

1 teaspoon baking soda

1 tablespoon ground ginger

1 teaspoon ground cinnamon

a good pinch of salt

1 extra-large egg, beaten

2 oz stem ginger, drained and finely chopped

To decorate

royal or glacé icing, or writing icing pens

mini-muffin pans lined with foil mini-muffin cases, or use double cases set on a baking sheet

MAKES ABOUT 36

Preheat the oven to 350°F.

Put the butter, molasses, honey, sugar, and milk in a saucepan over low heat and melt gently. Remove from the heat and let cool for a couple of minutes.

Meanwhile, sift the flour, baking soda, ground ginger, cinnamon, and salt into a mixing bowl. Pour in the cooled, melted mixture, then the egg. Mix thoroughly with a wooden spoon. Mix in the stem ginger.

Spoon the mixture into the cases using 2 teaspoons. Bake in the preheated oven for 15 minutes until firm to the touch.

Let cool on a wire rack, then decorate with icing. Store in an airtight container and eat within 3 days.

A QUICK AND EASY RECIPE WITH A RICH FLAVOR.
AND SINCE ALMOST EVERYONE LOVES FUDGE, AN
OFFERING OF A FEW SQUARES OF THIS WILL PUT
A SMILE ON ANYONE'S FACE.

Chocolate and cream fudge

3½ oz bittersweet chocolate,
coarsely chopped

4 tablespoons unsalted butter,
diced

2 tablespoons heavy cream

1 teaspoon pure vanilla extract
or dark rum

1 tablespoon light corn syrup

scant 2 cups confectioners'
sugar, sifted

*a shallow, 8-inch square pan,
greased*

MAKES 20 SQUARES

Melt the chocolate and butter in a heatproof bowl set over a pan of steaming but not boiling water. Do not let the base of the bowl touch the water. Stir frequently until melted, then remove the bowl from the heat and gently stir in the cream, then the vanilla extract, followed by the corn syrup.

Using a wooden spoon, then your hands, work in the confectioners' sugar 1 tablespoon at a time, to make a thick, smooth fudge. If the mixture starts to stiffen before all the sugar has been incorporated, return the bowl to the heat for a minute or so.

Transfer the mixture to the prepared pan and press in evenly. Chill until firm, then turn out and cut into squares with a large, sharp knife. Keep in the fridge and eat within 10 days.

THIS RECIPE IS GREAT FOR CHRISTMAS AS THE ROUND
TRUFFLES CAN BE LEFT PLAIN OR DECORATED WITH
SCRAPS OF RED AND GREEN COLORED SUGAR PASTE
(OR READY-ROLL ICING) TO LOOK LIKE HOLLY BERRIES
AND LEAVES, OR WITH ROYAL ICING (SEE PAGE 15)
TO RESEMBLE A TRADITIONAL BRITISH 'CANNON BALL'
CHRISTMAS PUDDING. YOU CAN ALSO ADD A SPLASH
OF BRANDY OR RUM TO THE MIXTURE.

Christmas truffles

**8 oz bittersweet chocolate,
coarsely chopped**

**4½ oz (1 cup) chocolate
spongecake crumbs**

⅔ cup ground almonds

**unsweetened cocoa powder,
to dust**

foil petits-fours or mini-muffin cases

Melt the chocolate in a heatproof bowl set over a pan of steaming
but not boiling water. Do not let the base of the bowl touch the
water. Stir occasionally until melted, then remove the bowl from
the heat.

Stir in the spongecake crumbs and ground almonds. When
thoroughly combined, cover the bowl and chill until firm, about
30 minutes. The mixture can be kept in the fridge, tightly covered,
for up to 3 days.

Using a teaspoon of mixture for each truffle, roll the mixture into
neat balls with your hands, then drop into a small bowl of cocoa
and shake to lightly coat. Set each truffle in a foil case. Chill until
firm, then pack into boxes or store in an airtight container. Keep in
a cool place or the fridge and and eat within 1 week.

Savory treats

IT'S HARD TO EAT JUST ONE OF THESE CRISP, SAVORY
CRACKERS, SO THEY'RE PERFECT WITH DRINKS AT
PARTY TIME, OR WITH A BOWL OF SOUP. THE RECIPE
COMES FROM ALYSON COOK, WHO CATERS TO THE
STARS OF HOLLYWOOD.

Parmesan herb crisps

3½ oz Parmesan or
Grana Padano cheese, grated

1 cup all-purpose flour

1 stick unsalted butter,
chilled and diced

½ teaspoon dried
herbes de Provence

½ teaspoon Worcestershire
sauce

2 tablespoons white wine
(optional)

baking parchment
2 baking sheets, greased

MAKES 50–60

Put all the ingredients in a food processor and blend until the
mixture forms a ball of dough.

Remove the dough from the processor and put on a sheet of
nonstick baking parchment. Shape into a log about 12 x 1 inch.
Wrap tightly in plastic wrap, then chill until firm, about 2 hours.
The mixture can be kept in the fridge, tightly wrapped, for up
to 4 days.

When ready to cook, preheat the oven to 375°F.

Cut the log into ¼-inch slices. Arrange the slices well apart on
the prepared baking sheets and bake in the preheated oven for
12–15 minutes until light golden.

Let cool on the baking sheets for 2 minutes, then transfer the
crisps to a wire rack to cool completely. Store in an airtight
container and eat within 5 days or freeze for up to 1 month.

THESE ATTRACTIVE SAVORY COOKIES FROM FRANCE ARE MADE FROM
PUFF PASTRY FOLDED UP WITH A MIXTURE OF CHEESE AND MUSTARD,
AND ARE QUITE SIMPLE TO ASSEMBLE. CHOOSE THE ALL-BUTTER KIND
OF READY-MADE PASTRY FOR THE BEST FLAVOR AND FLAKINESS.

Cheese palmiers

4 oz Parmesan or Grana Padano
cheese, finely grated

12 oz all-butter puff pastry,
thawed if necessary

1 tablespoon Dijon mustard

½ teaspoon mild paprika

¼ teaspoon cayenne pepper or
ground black pepper

*2 baking sheets, lined with
baking parchment*

MAKES 36

Sprinkle a little of the grated cheese on the work surface and gently unroll
the pastry, or if necessary, roll out to a rectangle about 9 x 15 inches.
Spread the mustard over the pastry with a round-bladed knife. Mix the rest
of the cheese with the paprika and pepper, then scatter over the pastry.

Now fold the pastry—it is supposed to resemble a palm leaf—but don't fold
too tightly or the pastry won't puff up in the oven. Fold each long side over
towards the center, then fold each side over again so there are 4 layers of
pastry on each side of the center. Then fold one folded side of pastry on top
of the other to make a log shape. Using a sharp knife, cut into slices about
¼ inch thick. Arrange the slices on the prepared baking sheets spaced well
apart to allow for spreading, and leave the 2 halves of the "U" shape slightly
open so the pastry can puff up.

Chill for 15 minutes. Meanwhile, preheat the oven to 425°F.

Bake in the preheated oven for 8–10 minutes until crisp, well-puffed, and
golden. Transfer to a wire rack and let cool. Store in an airtight container
and eat within 1 day—if necessary warm in a low oven before serving to
crisp up.

Sweet, sticky palmiers—Sprinkle the work surface with sugar and unroll or
roll out the pastry as above. Sprinkle with 3 tablespoons sugar mixed with
1 teaspoon ground cinnamon, then scatter over 2 tablespoons very finely
chopped pecans. Press the nuts lightly into the pastry. Fold the dough as
above and cut into slices, chill, and bake—they will brown quicker than
the cheese palmiers so watch them carefully.

RICHLY FLAVORED WITH GOOD SWISS CHEESE AND
SPIKED WITH DRIED HOT PEPPER FLAKES, THESE SMALL
CRISP PUFFS ARE DELICIOUS WITH A GLASS OF WINE OR
BOWL OF SOUP. THEY CAN BE BAKED A DAY OR SO IN
ADVANCE, THEN GENTLY WARMED BEFORE SERVING.

Spicy cheese gougères

5 tablespoons unsalted butter, diced

¼ teaspoon salt

¼–½ teaspoon dried hot pepper flakes, to taste

¾ cup all-purpose flour

3 extra-large eggs, beaten

4 oz Swiss cheese, finely diced, plus 1 oz, finely grated

2 baking sheets, greased and sprinkled with water

MAKES 40

Put the butter, salt, pepper flakes, and ¼ cup water into a medium pan. Heat gently until the butter has melted, then quickly bring to a boil. Remove the pan from the heat and tip in the flour. Beat well with a wooden spoon—don't worry that the mixture looks a mess to begin with as it will come together to make a smooth, shiny dough with a minute or so of vigorous beating. Return the pan to the heat and stir over low heat for 1 minute. Tip the dough into the bowl of an electric mixer and let cool completely.

When nearly cool, preheat the oven to 425°F.

Gradually beat the eggs into the cooled dough in the mixer, beating well after each addition. Stir in the diced cheese.

Using 2 teaspoons, spoon the mixture into small heaps of about a teaspoonful on the prepared baking sheets, spacing them well apart. Sprinkle with the finely grated cheese, then bake in the preheated oven for 10–15 minutes until golden brown and crisp.

Transfer the gougères to a wire rack and let cool. Store in an airtight container and eat within 3 days. Warm gently in the oven before serving.

CRISP, BUTTERY SAVORY CHEESE COOKIES SIMPLY MADE IN A FOOD PROCESSOR. SMOKED PAPRIKA ADDS AN INTRIGUING TASTE ALTHOUGH YOU COULD USE A LITTLE COARSELY GROUND BLACK PEPPER OR A VERY LITTLE RED-HOT CAYENNE PEPPER INSTEAD.

Walnut sablés

¼ cup all-purpose flour

7 tablespoons unsalted butter, chilled and diced

½ teaspoon smoked mild paprika

3½ oz Parmesan or Grana Padano cheese, finely grated

1 cup walnut pieces

1 extra-large egg yolk

1–2 baking sheets, lightly greased

MAKES 20

Put the flour, butter, paprika, and cheese into the bowl of a food processor. Run the machine until the mixture looks like fine crumbs. Add the nuts and the egg yolk and run the machine until the dough comes together into a ball.

Turn the dough out of the bowl, flour your hands and shape into a brick about 5 x 2½ x 2 inches. Wrap in plastic wrap and chill until firm, about 30 minutes. The mixture can be kept in the fridge, tightly wrapped, for up to 3 days.

When ready to continue, preheat the oven to 375°F.

Using a large, sharp knife, cut the brick of dough into 20 even slices. Arrange slightly apart on the prepared baking sheets, then bake in the preheated oven for 12–15 minutes until golden brown and just firm.

Remove the baking sheets from the oven and set on a wire rack. Let cool completely before lifting off the sablés. Store in an airtight container and eat within 3 days.

HOMEMADE BREAD STICKS LOOK AND TASTE SO MUCH BETTER THAN THE TYPE FROM THE SUPERMARKET. SERVE IN TALL GLASS PITCHERS FOR PARTIES ALONGSIDE DIPS, SPREADS, AND SOFT CHEESES. THE BASIC DOUGH IS DIVIDED INTO 3 AND INDIVIDUALLY FLAVORED.

Grissini

4 cups all-purpose flour

¼ oz active dry yeast

2 teaspoons sea salt

1½ cups tepid water

4 tablespoons olive oil

1 oz Parmesan or
Grana Padano cheese, grated

2 tablespoons sesame seeds

1 oz pitted black olives, chopped

2–3 baking sheeets, lightly greased

MAKES 36

Combine the flour, yeast, and salt in a large mixing bowl or the bowl of a large electric mixer. Make a well in the center and pour in the water and oil. Gradually work the ingredients together—use the dough hook attachment of the mixer on low speed—to make a fairly firm dough. If necessary, add a little more water or flour.

Turn out the dough onto a lightly floured work surface and knead for 10 minutes until very elastic or 5 minutes using the mixer.

Divide the dough into 3 portions. Add half the Parmesan to one portion and work in. Add half the sesame seeds to the second portion and work in. Finally, work all the chopped olives into the last portion.

Place each portion in a different bowl, cover, and leave in a warm place until doubled in size, about 1 hour.

When ready to continue, preheat the oven to 450°F.

Punch down each portion of dough, then knead for 30 seconds on a lightly floured work surface. Divide each portion of dough into 12 equal pieces. Using your hands, roll each to a thin sausage about 12 inches long. Arrange slightly apart on the prepared baking sheets. Lightly brush the grissini with water, then sprinkle the remaining cheese over the cheese grissini and the remaining sesame seeds over the sesame ones. Leave the olive grissini plain. Bake in the preheated oven for about 15 minutes until crisp and golden.

Transfer to a wire rack and let cool. Store in an airtight container and eat within 4 days. Gently warm in the oven before serving to crisp up.

Spicy nuts

THE GREAT THING ABOUT MAKING SPICY NUTS IS THAT THEY ARE ABSOLUTELY FRESH AND CRUNCHY AND YOU KNOW WHAT'S IN THE MIX. LOOK OUT FOR LARGE BAGS OF MIXED NUTS—CASHEWS, BRAZILS, ALMONDS, PECANS, HAZELNUTS, AND WALNUTS. ANY LEFTOVER NUTS CAN BE STIRRED INTO A PILAFF OR COUSCOUS.

2 tablespoons olive oil
12 oz unsalted mixed nuts
1 tablespoon light brown sugar
1 tablespoon Japanese soy sauce
¼–½ teaspoon cayenne pepper
¼–½ teaspoon ground black pepper
½ teaspoon smoked mild paprika

SERVES ABOUT 8

Heat the oil in a nonstick skillet. Add the nuts, stir well, then add all the other ingredients and stir-fry over medium heat for about 5 minutes until golden.

Tip into a heatproof bowl and let cool.

Serve the same day or store in an airtight container and eat within 2 days.

Marinated olives

OLIVES IN A DELICIOUS MARINADE CAN BE PART OF AN ANTIPASTI SPREAD, HANDED ROUND WITH DRINKS, OR ADDED TO PIZZAS AND SALADS. THE FLAVORED OIL CAN BE RECYCLED FOR DRESSINGS AND MARINADES.

9 oz black olives (Kalamata or Niçoise)
2 garlic cloves, thinly sliced
2 fresh rosemary sprigs
2 fresh thyme sprigs
2 fresh oregano sprigs
pared zest of 1 unwaxed lemon, in strips
good extra virgin olive oil, to cover

a sterilized glass jar and lid (see page 4)

SERVES ABOUT 8

Rinse the olives and drain well.

Put the garlic, sprigs of herbs, and strips of lemon zest into the sterilized jar with about 4 tablespoons of the olive oil. Close the jar and shake well. Open up the jar and add the olives, then close the jar and gently shake it again so the olives are well coated in the marinade. Open the jar and fill with enough oil to well cover the olives. Seal and shake gently, then keep in the fridge for 2 weeks to marinate before using. Once opened, keep in the fridge, immersed in oil, and eat within 7–10 days. Serve at room temperature.

Preserves

I ALWAYS MAKE A BATCH OF THIS JEWEL-BRIGHT RUBY
RELISH TO GO WITH OUR THANKSGIVING TURKEY—I
LOVE THE RICH, FRUITY AROMA THAT FILLS THE HOUSE
WHEN IT'S COOKING. IT GOES INTO THE SANDWICHES
WITH COLD TURKEY AND HAM, OR SIMPLY ALONGSIDE
SOME MATURE CHEDDAR. I TRY TO KEEP SOME FOR
CHRISTMAS BUT IT'S USUALLY ALL GONE BY THEN!

Cranberry and basil relish

2 tablespoons olive oil

1 medium red onion,
finely chopped

2 garlic cloves, crushed

12 oz fresh or frozen
cranberries (no need to thaw)

½ cup demerara sugar

¼ cup red wine vinegar

a small bunch of fresh basil,
leaves only

¼ teaspoon sea salt

several grinds of black pepper

*several sterilized glass jars and lids
(see page 4)*

MAKES 1¼ CUPS

Heat the olive oil in a large, heavy skillet or sauté pan, preferably
nonstick. Add the onion and garlic and cook gently, stirring
occasionally, for 5 minutes.

Add the rest of the ingredients to the pan and stir well. Cook over
medium heat, stirring frequently, until very thick, about 10 minutes.
Taste and adjust the seasoning, adding more salt or pepper as
needed. Spoon into the sterilized jars and seal. When completely
cold, keep in the fridge and use within 1 month.

A BRIGHT AND ZINGY RELISH THAT CAN BE MADE AT ANY TIME OF THE YEAR, HOWEVER IT IS PARTICULARLY GOOD WITH COLD HAM AND CHEESE, SO IT MAKES AN EXCELLENT PRESENT AT HOLIDAY TIME.

Ginger fruit relish

5 medium or large unwaxed oranges

2 pears

2 apples, fairly tart

6 tablespoons white wine vinegar

1¼ cups light brown sugar

2 inches fresh ginger, peeled and grated

1 teaspoon sea salt

¼ cup raisins

grated zest and freshly squeezed juice of 1 unwaxed lemon

several sterilized glass jars and lids (see page 4)

MAKES ABOUT 3½ CUPS

Rinse the oranges, then grate the zest and reserve. Using a serrated knife, peel the oranges to remove all the skin and the white pith. Cut into small chunks, discarding the pips.

Peel and core the pears and apples, and cut into chunks the same size as the oranges.

Put the vinegar and sugar into a large, heavy, nonaluminum pan and heat gently, stirring frequently to dissolve the sugar.

Add the grated ginger and salt to the pan. Bring to the boil, then stir in the chopped fruit. Boil gently for 20 minutes, stirring frequently until the fruit is very soft.

Stir in the reserved orange zest, the raisins, and the grated lemon zest and juice.

Cook for another 10–15 minutes, stirring frequently, until very thick and no longer watery on top.

Remove the pan from the heat and stir well. Spoon into the sterilized jars and seal. Let cool, then store in a cool spot for up to 1 month. Once opened, keep in the fridge.

A SLIGHTLY SPICY, SWEET GOLDEN SPREAD FOR
BREAKFAST MUFFINS, BRIOCHE, TOAST, OR WARM
BREAD ROLLS. IF YOU LIKE THE WARM, LEMONY
FLAVOR OF PRESERVED GINGER, ADD 1 OZ STEM
GINGER, DRAINED AND FINELY CHOPPED, RIGHT
AT THE END OF THE COOKING TIME.

Maple squash butter

2¼ lb butternut squash
½ cup pure apple juice
½–1 teaspoon ground ginger,
to taste
½ cup pure maple syrup
a cinnamon stick

*several sterilized glass jars and lids
(see page 4)*

MAKES 2½ CUPS

Preheat the oven to 350°F.

Halve the squash then scoop out the seeds. Set the two halves skin-side down in a baking dish. Cover tightly with foil, then bake in the preheated oven until tender, about 1¼–1½ hours.

Remove the squash from the oven and leave until cool enough to handle. Peel off the skin and dice the flesh. Put the flesh into the bowl of a food processor with the apple juice, ground ginger, and maple syrup and process until smooth.

Tip the purée into a heavy pan, add the cinnamon stick, and set over medium heat. Bring to a boil, then cook until very thick, about 10 minutes, stirring very frequently to prevent the mixture from sticking.

Spoon into the sterilized jars and seal. Let cool, then keep in the fridge and use within 2 weeks.

FROZEN RED FRUITS ARE AVAILABLE ALL YEAR ROUND AND ALWAYS MAKE A USEFUL ADDITION TO THE FREEZER. THIS RECIPE, MADE WITH A LARGE BAG CONTAINING RASPBERRIES, STRAWBERRIES, CHERRIES, BLUEBERRIES, RED CURRANTS, AND BLACK CURRANTS, MAKES A JUICY, THICK CONSERVE TO SERVE WARM OR AT ROOM TEMPERATURE WITH PANCAKES AND WAFFLES, ICE CREAM, MUFFINS, AND TOASTED BRIOCHE.

Red fruit conserve

2¼ lb frozen unsweetened red fruits

2 cups sugar

1 tablespoon lemon juice

1 cup red currant jelly

several sterilized glass jars and lids (see page 4)

MAKES 5 CUPS

Put the frozen fruits, sugar, lemon juice, and red currant jelly into a large nonmetallic bowl. Cover and leave for 2–4 hours, or overnight in the fridge, until the fruit has thawed.

Tip the mixture into a large, heavy, nonaluminum pan and bring to a boil. Simmer steadily until the mixture has thickened, about 10 minutes. Remove the pan from the heat, stir gently, then spoon into the sterilized jars and seal. Let cool, then keep in the fridge for up to 2 weeks.

Suppliers

American Spoon
www.spoon.com
Tel: 888-735-6700
*For plump, moist, chewy and tangy
dried cranberries and dried tart red
cherries, as well as other dried fruit.*

Buchanan Hollow Nut Company
www.bhnc.com
Tel: 1-800-532-1500
*For organic almonds and pistachios,
check out California's Buchanan
Hollow Nut Company.*

Confectionery House
www.confectioneryhouse.com
Tel: 518-279-4250
*Paper muffin cases in every color for
every occasion as well as sprinkles and
other edible decorations.*

Crafty Ribbons
www.craftyribbons.com
Every kind of ribbon imaginable.

Crate & Barrel
www.crateandbarrel.com
Tel: 800-967-6696
*Fill your kitchen with top-grade
bakeware, cookie cutters or even a
cookie press and decorating kit!*

Into the Oven
www.intotheoven.com
*For rolled fondant icing, dragées, edible
glitter dust, and other baking supplies.*

King Arthur Flour
www.kingarthurflour.com
Tel: 800-827-6836
*This site is an excellent resource for
baking supplies—cookie sheets, shaped
cookie molds, seasonal baking pans,
edible decorations, as well as the best
range of flours for all baking.*

Kitchen Krafts
www.kitchenkrafts.com
Tel: 800-298-5389
*The Foodcrafters Supply Catalog
carries cookie cutters, decorative jelly
jars, fun seasonal paper muffin cases,
food coloring etc.*

La Cuisine
www.lacuisineus.com
Tel: 1-800-521-1176
*La Cuisine, the Cook's Resource stocks
a large selection of handcrafted,
whimsical tinware cookie cutters from
Hammersong, as well as a wide range
fine baking equipment and ingredients.*

Nordic Ware
www.nordicware.com
Tel: 1-877-466-7342
*Family-owned bakeware manufacturer
which offers all sorts of shaped baking
pans and holiday cookie cutters.*

Offray
www.offray.com
Ribbons, ribbons and more ribbons.

Penzeys Spices
www.penzeys.com
*The holidays are a perfect time to
replenish your spice cupboard. Visit
Penzeys for best-quality vanilla,
cinnamon, nutmeg, cloves and more,
plus Spanish or Kashmir saffron for
your Saffron Cake.*

Squires Shop
www.squires-shop.com
*Online specialist suppliers of all things
to do with cakes, including decorating,
food coloring and sugarcraft.*

Sunnyland Farms
www.sunnylandfarms.com
Tel: 1-800-999-2488
*For very fresh, very fine pecans and
walnuts, go to Albany, Georgia's
Sunnyland Farms.*

Williams-Sonoma
www.williams-sonoma.com
Tel: 877-812-6235
*Beautiful selection of bakeware, such as
pans, cutters, baking sheets etc., plus
personalized ribbons and cellophane
bags for gift wrapping.*

Wilton
www.wilton.com
*Professional cake decorators know
Wilton, and baking enthusiasts at every
level will enjoy browsing their extensive
online store.*

Conversion chart

Weights and measures have been rounded up or down slightly to make measuring easier.

Measuring butter:

A US stick of butter weighs 4 oz which is approximately 115 g or 8 tablespoons.

Volume equivalents:

American	Metric	Imperial
1 teaspoon	5 ml	
1 tablespoon	15 ml	
¼ cup	60 ml	2 fl oz
⅓ cup	75 ml	2½ fl oz
½ cup	125 ml	4 fl oz
⅔ cup	150 ml	5 fl oz (¼ pint)
¾ cup	175 ml	6 fl oz
1 cup	250 ml	8 fl oz

Weight equivalents: **Measurements:**

Imperial	Metric	Inches	Cm
1 oz	30 g	¼ inch	5 mm
2 oz	55 g	½ inch	1 cm
3 oz	85 g	¾ inch	1.5 cm
3½ oz	100 g	1 inch	2.5 cm
4 oz	115 g	2 inches	5 cm
5 oz	140 g	3 inches	7 cm
6 oz	175 g	4 inches	10 cm
8 oz (½ lb)	225 g	5 inches	12 cm
9 oz	250 g	6 inches	15 cm
10 oz	280 g	7 inches	18 cm
11½ oz	325 g	8 inches	20 cm
12 oz	350 g	9 inches	23 cm
13 oz	375 g	10 inches	25 cm
14 oz	400 g	11 inches	28 cm
15 oz	425 g	12 inches	30 cm
16 oz (1 lb)	450 g		

Oven temperatures:

150°C	300°F	Gas 2
170°C	325°F	Gas 3
180°C	350°F	Gas 4
190°C	375°F	Gas 5
200°C	400°F	Gas 6

Index